"Zen Your Work Space: Mindful Strategies for Home Office Success"

Aura Marx

Introduction

In an era where the line between work and home has blurred, creating a sanctuary for productivity and peace in our home offices has never been more crucial. "Zen Your Work Space: Mindful Strategies for Home Office Success" is your companion in weaving the art of mindfulness into the fabric of your work life. Imagine starting each day in a workspace that doesn't just beckon you to tasks and deadlines but also invites you to breathe, focus, and thrive amidst the chaos.

At its core, this book is about converting your workplace into a place of mindfulness and productivity that brings calm and efficiency. What is mindfulness in the workplace, and why is it the key to a peaceful and productive home office? We'll answer these questions and explain how being present and engaged can improve work and you..

For Gen Xers and Millennials, the home office isn't just a trend; it's a significant part of our work-life narrative. Many of us have transitioned from traditional office settings to carving out workspaces in our living quarters. This shift presents unique challenges—from navigating distractions and setting boundaries to maintaining motivation without the buzz of office life. Yet, it also offers unparalleled opportunities for personalizing our work environments and integrating work with our broader life goals in a harmonious way.

This book is more than just a guide; it's a journey into reimagining what your workday can look like when you infuse it with mindfulness. Whether you're a seasoned remote worker or newly adapting to a home office setup, the strategies and insights shared here will help you navigate the complexities of working from home while safeguarding your well-being and productivity. As we embark on this journey together, remember that creating a mindful workspace is not about achieving perfection; it's about embracing progress, one mindful moment at a time. Let's redefine what it means to work from home and transform your workspace into a haven of balance, peace, and productivity.

Table of Contents

Chapter 1: Understanding Mindfulness

Imagine starting your day not with the buzzing of an alarm, but with the gentle awareness of your own breathing. Picture yourself navigating through tasks with a sense of calm and focus, undisturbed by the ebb and flow of daily distractions. This is the essence of mindfulness—a simple yet profound practice that has the power to transform not just your workday but your entire life.

At its heart, mindfulness is about being fully present in the moment, engaging with our experiences without judgment or distraction. It's a practice rooted in ancient traditions, most notably Buddhism, where it forms part of the path to enlightenment. But mindfulness isn't about changing our thoughts; it's about changing our relationship with our thoughts. It's about noticing when our mind has wandered and gently guiding it back to the present.

In our modern context, mindfulness has been distilled into a secular, accessible practice, relevant to everyone, irrespective of background or belief. Its simplicity is deceptive, for within this practice lies the key to untold depths of peace and clarity.

The journey of mindfulness from monastic settings to mainstream society is a fascinating tale of adaptation and rediscovery. Pioneers like Jon Kabat-Zinn played a pivotal role in this transition, introducing mindfulness in a clinical context with the Mindfulness-Based Stress Reduction (MBSR) program. This marked a turning point, bringing the therapeutic benefits of mindfulness to a wider audience and sparking a global movement of awareness.

In today's fast-paced, digitally saturated world, the need for mindfulness has never been greater. The constant barrage of notifications, the endless to-do lists, and the pressure to multitask have fragmented our attention, leaving us feeling drained and disconnected. Mindfulness offers a sanctuary—a way to reclaim our focus and nurture a state of calm amid the chaos.

Research has illuminated the profound impact of mindfulness on mental and physical health, highlighting its ability to reduce stress, enhance cognitive function, and improve emotional resilience. In the realm of work, particularly in home offices where the personal and professional often merge, mindfulness can be a lifeline, helping us navigate the demands of our jobs with grace and efficiency.

Mindfulness and Productivity: An Unlikely Alliance

At first glance, mindfulness and productivity might seem like strange bedfellows. How can a practice rooted in being present and slowing down align with the goal of getting more done? The answer lies in the quality of our attention. Mindfulness cultivates a laser-like focus, enabling us to engage deeply with our work without getting overwhelmed. It teaches us to handle interruptions with equanimity and to approach each task with a fresh perspective.

Integrating mindfulness into your workspace starts with small, intentional steps. It might be as simple as beginning your day with a minute of deep breathing or setting reminders to pause and check in with yourself throughout the day. It's about creating an environment that supports focus and presence, whether through decluttering your desk, introducing elements of nature, or ensuring your workspace promotes comfort and well-being.

Embarking on Your Mindfulness Journey
As you embark on this journey of integrating mindfulness into your work life, remember that the goal is not to add another item to your to-do list. Mindfulness is a way of being, a lens through which you can experience the world more fully. It's about finding joy in the mundane, peace in the midst of deadlines, and clarity amid confusion.

In the chapters that follow, we'll explore practical strategies for weaving mindfulness into the fabric of your workday, transforming your home office into a haven of productivity and tranquility. Together, we'll discover how the ancient practice of mindfulness can illuminate the path to a more fulfilling and balanced work life in the modern world.

Chapter 2: The Evolution of the Home Office

A Space of One's Own

Once a rarity, the home office has woven itself into the fabric of our daily lives, becoming as familiar as the living room or kitchen. This transformation didn't happen overnight but evolved through a confluence of technology, culture, and necessity, forever altering how Gen Xers and Millennials view and engage with work.

In the past, the concept of a home office was often reserved for writers, artists, or entrepreneurs—those whose work naturally fit into the domestic sphere. For many, the very idea of working from home was a novelty, a break from the norm that suggested a lifestyle of flexibility and autonomy that was more aspiration than reality.

The Digital Revolution: Blurring the Lines

The advent of the internet and digital communication technologies marked a turning point in this evolution. Suddenly, the tools and connections needed to perform a vast array of jobs were as accessible in the spare bedroom as they were in the corporate office. This digital revolution didn't just make remote work possible; it made it practical, efficient, and, for many, preferable.

For Gen X and Millennials, the rise of the home office coincided with a broader reevaluation of work and life priorities. These generations, more than those before them, value work-life balance, flexibility, and the freedom to blend personal and professional pursuits. The home office, with its inherent adaptability, became not just a workspace but a symbol of a new way of working—one that challenges the traditional 9-to-5 and the physical boundaries of the office.

Millennials, in particular, have been at the forefront of this shift. More than just a place to work, they see the home office as an extension of their identity and values—a space where work is meaningful and aligned with personal goals and well-being. This perspective has reshaped expectations around work environments, driving demand for flexibility, technology integration, and environments that foster creativity and well-being.

The Global Office: Connectivity and Community

As home offices became more prevalent, they also became more connected. The world shrank into a global office, where teams collaborate across continents and time zones from the comfort of their homes. This connectivity brought about new communities of remote workers, sharing strategies, challenges, and triumphs, further embedding the home office into the mainstream work culture.

The COVID-19 pandemic accelerated the home office evolution in unprecedented ways. What was once a choice became a necessity for millions, as lockdowns and social distancing measures forced a global experiment in remote work. This period of forced adaptation demonstrated the viability of widespread remote work, pushing companies and individuals to rethink the necessity of physical offices and embrace the flexibility of home-based setups.

The Future Is Flexible: A Hybrid Model Emerges
In the wake of the pandemic, a new hybrid work model has emerged, blending remote and in-office work. This model acknowledges the benefits of home offices while recognizing the value of physical spaces for collaboration and community. It's a testament to the enduring legacy of the home office—a space that has evolved from a novel concept to a cornerstone of modern work life.

As we navigate this ongoing evolution, the home office remains a dynamic space, reflective of our individual needs, work styles, and the changing landscape of work itself. For Gen X and Millennials, it's a space that offers not just a place to work, but an opportunity to redefine what work means, blending productivity with personal well-being, and in doing so, crafting a work life that is not only successful but truly fulfilling.

Chapter 3: Zen Your Physical Space

Transforming your home office into a Zen sanctuary is about more than aesthetics; it's about creating an environment that nurtures your well-being and enhances your ability to focus and create. This chapter will guide you through decluttering, organizing, and personalizing your space with an emphasis on mindfulness and intentionality.

Decluttering is the cornerstone of a Zen workspace. It's not just about tidying up; it's a mindful exercise in letting go of what no longer serves you, both physically and mentally. Begin by evaluating each item in your office. Ask yourself: Does this spark creativity? Is it essential for my work? Does it bring me joy or peace? If the answer is no, it may be time to let it go. This process clears not only your physical space but also your mental clutter, paving the way for clarity and focus.

Mindful Organizing

With decluttering complete, organizing your space becomes a canvas for your mindfulness practice. Each object in your office should have a purpose and a place. Use organizers, trays, and bins to keep essential items accessible yet orderly. Consider the flow of your workday and arrange your tools accordingly. This intentional organization minimizes distractions, allowing you to flow seamlessly from one task to the next with a calm and focused mind.

The Palette of Tranquility

Colors have a profound impact on our emotions and energy levels. To infuse your office with tranquility and focus, opt for a palette inspired by nature. Soft greens evoke the serenity of a lush forest, gentle blues mirror the calming presence of the sky, and earth tones ground you with their warmth and stability. These hues create a backdrop of peace, making your office a haven from the bustling world outside.

Embracing Nature's Touch

Incorporating natural elements into your workspace is like opening a window to the outdoors, inviting an essence of harmony and vitality. A simple potted plant can transform your desk, bringing life and freshness to your space. Natural light is equally transformative; it uplifts your spirit and enhances your energy. If possible, position your desk where you can bask in the glow of natural light, and if not, consider daylight-simulating lamps to capture that same invigorating essence.

Ergonomics: The Foundation of Comfort

Mindfulness extends to the physical realm through ergonomics. An ergonomically designed workspace respects your body's natural posture, reducing strain and fostering physical ease. Invest in a chair that supports your spine, a desk at the right height, and a computer setup that prevents unnecessary strain. This alignment between your body and your workspace not only enhances comfort but also keeps you grounded and present in your work.

A Symphony of Senses

Your office should cater to all your senses, creating a symphony that inspires peace and productivity. Soft, ambient music or the gentle sound of a water feature can soothe the mind and mask distracting sounds. Aromatherapy, with scents like lavender for calmness or peppermint for alertness, can set the mood for your workday. Even the tactile experience of your office—be it the smoothness of your desk surface or the comfort of your chair—plays a role in your overall sense of well-being.

Personal Touches of Joy

While minimalism is a key aspect of a Zen space, personal touches that spark joy are equally important. These should be chosen with intention, whether it's artwork that inspires, a family photo that brings a smile, or a keepsake that centers you. These items are not mere decorations; they are touchstones that connect you to what matters most, grounding you in the present.

Creating Your Zen Rituals

As you enter and leave your office, consider establishing rituals that signify the start and end of your workday. This might be a moment of deep breathing, a few stretches, or lighting a candle. These rituals demarcate your work time, helping you transition into and out of your work mode with mindfulness and intention.

Your Workspace, Your Zen Sanctuary

Creating a Zen office is a journey of curating a space that aligns with your inner state, fostering an environment where clarity, peace, and productivity flourish. As you implement these strategies, remember that this is your personal sanctuary. It should reflect your unique path to mindfulness and productivity, serving as a space where you can truly thrive in your work and in your well-being.

Chapter 4: Ergonomics and Mindfulness

Harmony Between Body and Mind

Creating a workspace that marries ergonomics with mindfulness is about fostering an environment where comfort and ease pave the way for deep focus and presence. This chapter will guide you through setting up an ergonomic workspace that not only supports your physical well-being but also enhances your mental clarity and mindfulness practice.

The Ergonomic Foundation: Aligning Your Space

The foundation of an ergonomic workspace is alignment—between your body, your furniture, and your work tools. This alignment minimizes physical strain, allowing your body to maintain a natural and comfortable posture throughout the day. Begin with a chair that supports the natural curve of your spine, adjustable in height so your feet can rest flat on the ground. Your desk should be at a height where your elbows can rest comfortably at a 90-degree angle, and your computer monitor should be at eye level to prevent neck strain.

Mindfulness in Movement: The Dynamic Workspace

An ergonomic workspace encourages movement, breaking the monotony of prolonged sitting which can lead to discomfort and distractibility. Consider a sit-stand desk that allows you to alternate between sitting and standing, integrating gentle movement into your workday. This variability in posture not only supports physical health but also keeps the mind alert and engaged, fostering a state of mindfulness.

The Power of Pause: Integrating Mindful Breaks
Ergonomics isn't just about how you sit or stand; it's also about how you pause. Regular breaks are essential to prevent fatigue and maintain a state of mindfulness. Use these pauses to practice brief mindfulness exercises, such as deep breathing, stretching, or a short walk. These mindful breaks serve as resets, not just for your body but also for your mind, helping you return to your work with renewed focus and clarity.

Creating a Sensory Environment for Mindfulness
An ergonomic workspace also caters to your senses, creating an environment that supports mindfulness. Ensure your lighting is adequate but not harsh, reducing eye strain and creating a calming atmosphere. Consider the textures and materials in your workspace; materials that evoke a sense of calm and comfort can enhance your mindfulness practice. The incorporation of plants or a view of nature can also soothe the senses and foster a deeper connection to the present moment.

The Sound of Mindfulness: Auditory Ergonomics
Sound plays a critical role in both ergonomics and mindfulness. In an ergonomic sense, reducing noise pollution is key to preventing auditory fatigue and maintaining concentration. From a mindfulness perspective, the sounds in your environment can either distract or deepen your presence. Explore soundscapes that enhance your mindfulness practice, whether it's calming music, nature sounds, or even the soothing hum of white noise, to create an auditory backdrop that supports deep focus and presence.

Ergonomic Tools: Extensions of Mindfulness
Ergonomic tools, from keyboards and mice to document holders and footrests, are not just physical supports but extensions of your mindfulness practice. These tools should not only reduce strain but also integrate seamlessly into your workflow, allowing you to maintain a mindful state of engagement with your work. Choose tools that feel intuitive and comfortable, reducing the mental effort required to use them and allowing you to stay present and focused.

Personalizing Your Ergonomic Mindfulness Practice
While there are general principles for setting up an ergonomic workspace, true harmony between ergonomics and mindfulness comes from personalization. Pay attention to your body's signals throughout the day and adjust your setup accordingly. This mindful attunement to your physical needs not only enhances comfort but also deepens your connection to your body and your work.

Mindfulness Beyond the Physical Space
Finally, remember that mindfulness in an ergonomic workspace extends beyond the physical setup. It's about cultivating an attitude of awareness and presence, regardless of the task at hand. Whether you're typing an email, participating in a virtual meeting, or brainstorming a new project, approach each activity with full attention and intention, embracing the ergonomic principles not just as a means to comfort but as a pathway to deeper mindfulness.

Your Workspace: A Mindful Ergonomic Sanctuary
By integrating ergonomics with mindfulness, your workspace becomes more than just a place to work; it becomes a sanctuary where body and mind are in harmony, where comfort and ease facilitate a state of deep focus and presence. As you refine your ergonomic setup and deepen your mindfulness practice, you'll discover a workspace that not only supports your physical well-being but also nurtures your mental and emotional health, transforming the act of work into an opportunity for mindfulness and growth.

Chapter 5: Mindful Starting Rituals

How you begin your workday sets the tone for everything that follows. Mindful starting rituals are about more than just productivity; they're about entering your workspace with a sense of purpose and presence. This chapter explores techniques to start your day with intention, grounding you in mindfulness and aligning your activities with your deeper goals.

Before diving into the day's tasks, allow yourself a moment of stillness. Begin with a simple mindfulness exercise upon waking or entering your office. This could be a few minutes of deep breathing, a short meditation, or a gentle stretch. The key is to anchor yourself in the present, acknowledging and releasing any lingering thoughts from sleep or previous days, and setting a clear, calm foundation for the day ahead.

With a clear mind, set your intentions for the day. Intentions differ from tasks; they're about the mindset and values you want to embody as you move through your tasks. Do you wish to approach your work with creativity, patience, or perhaps a spirit of collaboration? Writing down your intentions can solidify them, serving as a touchstone you can return to throughout the day to realign your actions with your deeper purpose.

While to-do lists are useful, they often become overwhelming catalogs of tasks that can lead to stress and distraction. Instead, adopt a mindful approach to goal setting. Select a few key tasks that align with your intentions and contribute meaningfully to your larger goals. For each task, consider why it's important and how it serves your broader objectives, infusing your work with purpose and direction.

Create a ritual for physically entering your workspace, whether it's opening a door, sitting down at your desk, or turning on your computer. Use this action as a cue to transition into work mode mindfully. Pause, take a deep breath, and consciously cross the threshold into your day's work, leaving behind any personal concerns or distractions.

Gratitude Practice: Starting with Positivity
Incorporate a brief gratitude practice into your morning ritual. Reflect on three things you're grateful for each morning, whether related to work or personal life. This practice can shift your mindset to one of positivity and abundance, fueling your day with a sense of contentment and motivation.

Mindful Movement: Energizing Your Start
Integrate a short session of mindful movement into your morning routine. This could be yoga, tai chi, or simply stretching—any gentle activity that connects your body and mind. This not only energizes you physically but also centers your focus, preparing you for the day's tasks with a sense of embodied awareness.

Mindful Consumption: Nourishing Your Mind and Body
Be mindful of your morning consumption, from the news you read to the food and drink you consume. Opt for nourishing choices that support your well-being and avoid overstimulating media that could set a tone of stress or negativity. A calming tea

or a healthy breakfast, consumed with presence, can be a soothing ritual that prepares you for the day ahead.

Digital Mindfulness: Setting Technological Boundaries
In our connected world, it's tempting to start the day by checking emails or social media. However, this can quickly lead to a reactive rather than intentional mindset. Set boundaries around digital devices in the morning, giving yourself a clear, undistracted space to engage with your starting rituals and intentions before diving into the digital world.

Reflective Journaling: Clarity through Writing
Consider starting your day with a few minutes of reflective journaling. This can be a space to explore your intentions, acknowledge any anxieties, and articulate your goals for the day. Writing provides clarity, turning abstract thoughts and feelings into concrete intentions and plans.

Your Morning, Your Ritual
These mindful starting rituals are not one-size-fits-all; they're meant to be adapted to fit your unique needs and lifestyle. Experiment with different practices, and notice what resonates with you and what truly enhances your sense of presence and purpose as you start your workday. The goal is to cultivate a morning routine that grounds you in mindfulness, aligns your actions with your intentions, and sets a positive, productive tone for the day ahead.

Chapter 6: Productivity Through Presence

The Paradox of Presence in Productivity
In a world that often equates productivity with multitasking and constant activity, the concept of presence—fully engaging in the task at hand—can seem counterintuitive. Yet, it's precisely this deep focus and engagement that unlocks true productivity. This chapter explores strategies to cultivate presence, transforming the way you work by enhancing both your efficiency and the quality of your output.

The Power of Single-Tasking
Our first strategy is a return to single-tasking. In an age of multitasking, the act of dedicating your full attention to one task at a time is revolutionary. Single-tasking allows for deeper immersion, creativity, and problem-solving. Start by identifying one task to focus on, eliminate potential distractions, and give yourself permission to fully engage with this singular task. Notice how this focused approach not only improves the quality of your work but also your satisfaction in doing it.

The Pomodoro Technique: Structured Focus
The Pomodoro Technique is a time management method that breaks work into intervals, traditionally 25 minutes in length, separated by short breaks. This technique encourages sustained focus and prevents burnout by pairing intense, undistracted work sessions with regular, restorative pauses. Each "Pomodoro" session is a commitment to presence, allowing you to dive deep into your work with the knowledge that a break is never too far away.

Mindful Breaks: Recharging with Intention

Breaks are not just pauses in your work; they're opportunities to recharge and reconnect with the present moment. During breaks, resist the urge to fill every moment with activity or digital engagement. Instead, practice mindfulness—whether through a brief meditation, a walk outside, or simply sitting quietly with a cup of tea. These mindful breaks refresh your mind and body, enhancing your ability to maintain presence throughout the workday.

Digital Detoxing: Reclaiming Your Focus

In our connected world, digital distractions are a constant challenge to presence. Digital detoxing—setting aside specific times to disconnect from digital devices—can help reclaim your focus. Designate times during your workday when you disconnect from emails, social media, and messaging. Use these periods for deep work, leveraging your undivided attention to make significant progress on challenging tasks.

Establishing boundaries is key to maintaining presence and focus. This includes setting clear work hours, communicating your availability to colleagues, and creating physical or virtual boundaries within your workspace. These boundaries help delineate your work time, allowing you to fully engage with your tasks without the constant pull of external demands.

Presence is not only about solitary work; it's also vital in interactions and communications. Practice mindful listening in meetings and conversations. Give your full attention to the speaker, resisting the urge to formulate your response while they're talking. This not only improves the quality of your interactions but also deepens your relationships and collaborations.

The Art of Noticing: Cultivating Awareness
Develop the habit of regularly checking in with yourself throughout the day. Pause to notice your breath, your posture, and your state of mind. This practice of noticing brings you back to the present moment, helping you become aware of when your focus has drifted and gently guiding it back to the task at hand.

Gratitude as a Focus Tool
Incorporating gratitude into your workday can enhance presence. Take moments to reflect on aspects of your work and environment that you're grateful for. This positive focus can transform your perspective, making it easier to engage fully with your tasks and find joy in the process.

Your physical workspace plays a significant role in supporting presence. Create an environment that minimizes distractions and promotes focus. This might include a clean and organized desk, noise-canceling headphones, or the strategic use of lighting and color to create a calm, focused atmosphere.

Presence as a Path to Productivity
By embracing these strategies, you're not just enhancing your productivity; you're transforming your relationship with work. Presence brings a quality of mindfulness to your tasks, turning each moment of your workday into an opportunity for engagement, satisfaction, and excellence. As you integrate these

practices into your daily routine, you'll find that productivity through presence is not only more enjoyable but also more sustainable and fulfilling.

Chapter 7: Mindful Communication

In the realm of remote work, communication is the lifeline that connects us to our colleagues, bridging distances and digital divides. Mindful communication goes beyond the mere exchange of information; it's about fostering understanding, empathy, and connection. This chapter delves into strategies for cultivating clear and compassionate communication in a remote setting, ensuring that our words and actions build bridges rather than barriers.

Begin each communication with a clear intention. What is the purpose of your message? Are you seeking to inform, request, or connect? By clarifying your intention, you can tailor your communication to be more effective and mindful, ensuring that your message is not just heard but understood.

Active Listening: The Foundation of Mindfulness

Mindful communication is as much about listening as it is about speaking. Practice active listening by giving your full attention to the speaker, free from distractions or the urge to multitask. Reflect on what is being said, both verbally and non-verbally, and resist the temptation to formulate your response while the other person is still speaking. This level of presence not only enhances understanding but also conveys respect and value to the speaker. In the absence of physical cues, conveying empathy in digital communication becomes crucial. Use empathetic language to acknowledge the feelings and perspectives of your colleagues. Phrases like "I understand where you're coming from" or "It sounds like that was a challenging situation" can go a long way in building rapport and trust.

Clarity and Brevity: The Art of Succinct Communication
In a digital landscape where attention is fragmented, clarity and brevity become vital. Be concise in your communication, avoiding unnecessary jargon or lengthy explanations that might dilute your message. Clear, direct communication respects the recipient's time and cognitive load, making it easier for them to engage and respond.

The Tone of Compassion
Tone can be challenging to convey in written communication, where nuances can easily be lost or misinterpreted. Be mindful of the tone you use in emails, messages, and even in video calls. A friendly greeting, expressions of gratitude, and words of encouragement can imbue your communications with warmth, fostering a positive and supportive team environment.

Video calls have become a staple of remote work, offering a visual connection in a digital world. Approach these calls with mindfulness, ensuring you're present and engaged. Simple actions like making eye contact (by looking at the camera), nodding, and smiling can significantly enhance the sense of connection and attentiveness in these interactions.

In moments of misunderstanding or conflict, take a mindful pause before responding. This space allows you to process your emotions and approach the situation with a calm, clear perspective. A thoughtful response, rather than a reactive one, can prevent escalation and foster mutual understanding.

Asking questions is a powerful tool in mindful communication. Inquire with genuine curiosity and an open mind, seeking to understand rather than to challenge or criticize. Mindful questions encourage dialogue and can lead to deeper insights and solutions.

Setting Boundaries for Communication
Mindful communication also involves setting and respecting boundaries. Clearly communicate your availability and preferred channels for different types of communication. Respecting these boundaries not only prevents burnout but also ensures that communication remains purposeful and effective.
The Practice of Regular Check-ins
Establish a routine of regular check-ins with your team or colleagues. These can be brief, focused meetings or informal virtual coffee chats. The goal is to maintain a human connection, share updates, and address any concerns in a relaxed, open setting.

Cultivating a Culture of Mindful Communication
Ultimately, mindful communication is about cultivating a culture of openness, respect, and empathy. Encourage practices that promote this culture, such as expressing appreciation, acknowledging achievements, and offering support. In a remote work environment, these gestures of mindfulness can significantly strengthen team cohesion and morale.

Chapter 8: Mindfulness Breaks

In the rhythm of a busy workday, especially in the solitude of a home office, breaks can become an afterthought—quick, distracted moments sandwiched between tasks. Yet, these pauses hold the potential for profound renewal, not just for our focus and energy but for our overall well-being. This chapter explores the art of mindfulness breaks—short, intentional practices that can transform these interludes into wellsprings of calm and clarity.

Breathing Exercises: The Core of Mindfulness

The simplest and perhaps most powerful mindfulness practice is focused on our breath. A brief breathing exercise can be a sanctuary of calm in the midst of a hectic day. Try the "4-7-8" technique: inhale deeply through your nose for 4 seconds, hold your breath for 7 seconds, and exhale slowly through your mouth for 8 seconds. This practice can quickly reduce stress and recenter your mind, making it an ideal start to any break.

Mindful Movement: Rejuvenation Through Gentle Activity

Incorporating mindful movement into your breaks can counteract the physical and mental stagnation of prolonged sitting. Gentle stretches, yoga poses, or tai chi movements can be performed in a small space and offer a dual benefit of relaxing the body and clearing the mind. Approach these movements with full attention, focusing on the sensations in your body and the rhythm of your breath, turning the activity into a moving meditation.

Nature Connection: The Outdoors as a Mindful Refuge

If possible, spend part of your break outdoors. A short walk in nature, or simply standing outside to feel the sun and breeze, can be incredibly restorative. Engage all your senses—notice the colors, sounds, and smells around you, and feel the ground beneath your feet. This sensory immersion can ground you in the present moment, offering a powerful contrast to the digital confines of work.

Guided Meditation: A Guided Journey to Calm

For those new to meditation or looking for a structured break, guided meditations can be a helpful tool. Numerous apps and online resources offer short meditations tailored to a variety of needs, from stress reduction to energy boosting. Even a few minutes spent in guided meditation can help reset your mental state, leaving you refreshed and ready to return to work with renewed focus.

Mindful Eating: Nourishment as a Practice

Turn a snack or a cup of tea into a mindfulness exercise by practicing mindful eating. Rather than eating while distracted by work or screens, focus solely on the experience of eating. Notice the flavors, textures, and sensations, and eat slowly, savoring each bite or sip. This practice not only enhances the enjoyment of your food but also fosters a deeper connection to the present moment.

Gratitude Reflection: Cultivating a Positive Mindset

Dedicate a few minutes of your break to reflect on what you're grateful for. You can jot down three things in a gratitude journal or simply pause to contemplate them. This practice shifts your focus from stressors and challenges to the positive aspects of your life, cultivating a mindset that can transform your approach to work and challenges.

Digital Detox: A Break from Screens

Consider making at least one of your daily breaks a complete digital detox—no screens, no notifications, just you and the moment. This can be a time for one of the previously mentioned activities or simply a moment of silence and stillness. The absence of digital distractions allows your mind a true respite, reducing cognitive overload and fostering a sense of inner peace.

Mindful Art: Creativity as a Mindful Exercise

Engaging in a creative activity, like doodling, coloring, or simple crafting, can be a meditative and rejuvenating break. The focus required for artistic creation can act as a form of mindfulness, drawing your attention away from work-related thoughts and into the flow of the present moment.

Mindful Listening: Soundscape Immersion

Dedicate a break to mindful listening. This could be listening to calming music, nature sounds, or even the ambient sounds of your environment. Close your eyes and let yourself fully engage with the auditory experience, noticing the nuances and textures of the sounds. This practice can be surprisingly restorative, offering a mental reset.

The Personal Touch: Customizing Your Mindfulness Breaks

The most effective mindfulness breaks are those that resonate personally with you. Experiment with different practices to find what best helps you to disconnect, refresh, and refocus. Remember, the goal is not to fill your break with activity but to provide a mindful pause that rejuvenates your mind and spirit.

Transforming Breaks into Pillars of Mindfulness
By integrating these mindfulness exercises into your breaks, you transform mere pauses into profound opportunities for renewal and self-care. These mindful breaks become pillars that support not just your productivity but your overall well-being, enriching your workday with moments of calm, clarity, and connection to the present moment.

Chapter 9: Physical Wellness in the Home Office

Physical wellness is the bedrock upon which our mental and emotional well-being rests, especially in the context of remote work where the lines between personal and professional life can blur. This chapter explores practical strategies for weaving physical activity and healthy habits into the fabric of your workday, ensuring that your home office is not just a place of productivity but also a space of vitality and wellness.

The Dynamic Desk: Making Movement Part of Your Workflow
Integrating movement into your work routine is essential to counteract the sedentary nature of desk jobs. Consider a sit-stand desk or a convertible workstation that allows for regular transitions between sitting and standing. Even small changes, like placing a printer or trash bin farther from your desk, can encourage brief but frequent movement breaks, subtly infusing your day with physical activity.

Scheduled Movement Breaks: The Rhythm of Wellness
Set reminders to take short movement breaks every hour. These don't need to be long—just a few minutes of stretching, walking, or simple exercises can significantly impact your physical health and mental clarity. These scheduled pauses not only alleviate physical strain but also rejuvenate your focus, making them a key component of a productive and healthy workday.

Mindful Posture: The Art of Sitting Well
Being mindful of your posture is crucial for physical wellness in a home office setting. Invest in an ergonomic chair that supports your spine's natural curve, and be conscious of maintaining a neutral posture with your feet flat on the ground and your shoulders relaxed. Regular posture checks can prevent the aches and pains associated with prolonged sitting, ensuring that your work environment supports your physical well-being.

Eye Health: Protecting Your Vision in the Digital Age
In an era dominated by screens, protecting your eyes is more important than ever. Follow the 20-20-20 rule: every 20 minutes, take a 20-second break to look at something 20 feet away. This practice helps reduce eye strain and fatigue. Additionally, adjust the brightness and contrast of your screen to comfortable levels and consider blue light filters to minimize exposure to potentially harmful light frequencies.

Nutrition at the Desk: Fueling Your Body and Mind
Mindful eating habits are a cornerstone of physical wellness, particularly when working from home where kitchen access can lead to constant snacking. Plan your meals and snacks, focusing on nutritious, energy-boosting foods that sustain you throughout the day. Hydration is equally important; keep a water bottle at your desk to ensure you're drinking enough water, keeping your body hydrated and your mind sharp.

Home Office Fitness: Integrating Exercise into Your Space
Create a small, dedicated space for exercise in or near your home office. This could be as simple as a yoga mat and a set of

dumbbells or resistance bands. Incorporate short, focused exercise sessions into your day, whether it's a morning workout to energize you before work or a midday session to break up the day and boost your metabolism.

The Power of Nature: Outdoor Activities for Wellness
Whenever possible, take your breaks or even your meetings outdoors. Walking meetings, whether virtual with a headset or in-person if applicable, can be a fantastic way to combine physical activity with productivity. Even a brief walk outside can improve your mood, increase your creativity, and provide a much-needed change of scenery.

Mind-Body Practices: Yoga, Tai Chi, and Beyond
Incorporate mind-body practices such as yoga or tai chi into your daily routine. These practices not only improve flexibility and strength but also promote mental calmness and focus, making them an ideal complement to the demands of remote work. Even a short session can serve as a physical and mental reset, preparing you for the tasks ahead with renewed energy and clarity.

End-of-Day Unwind: Physical Activities to Mark the Transition
Create an end-of-day ritual involving physical activity to help transition out of work mode. This could be a workout, a bike ride, or a walk—anything that signals to your body and mind that the workday is over. This practice helps delineate work and personal time, allowing you to decompress and shift gears into your personal life with ease.

Building a Culture of Wellness in Remote Work
Encourage and participate in wellness challenges or activities with your remote team. This not only fosters a sense of community and shared purpose but also motivates you to stay committed to your physical wellness goals. Sharing tips, progress, and experiences can create a supportive environment that values and promotes wellness as a fundamental part of the remote work experience.

Chapter 10: Creating a Work-Life Boundary

The Art of Balance in the Remote Work Era

In the landscape of remote work, the lines between professional and personal life can often blur, leading to a world where work seeps into every corner of our lives. Establishing clear work-life boundaries is not just a matter of discipline; it's an essential practice for maintaining balance, well-being, and effectiveness. This chapter explores strategies to delineate these boundaries, ensuring that your home office serves as a productive workspace without overtaking your personal sanctuary.

The first step in creating a work-life boundary is establishing a designated workspace. Whether it's a separate room or a specific corner of a room, this physical demarcation signals to your brain that "this is where work happens." When you leave this space, it serves as a physical cue that work has ended, allowing you to transition more fully into personal time.

Cultivate rituals that mark the beginning and end of your workday. A morning ritual might involve setting intentions, reviewing your schedule, or a simple exercise routine. An evening ritual could be a reflection on the day's achievements, a closing meditation, or the act of shutting down your computer and organizing your desk. These rituals frame your workday, providing clear signals to your mind that work has commenced or concluded.

Technology plays a significant role in blurring work-life boundaries. Establish clear rules about technology use—set specific times to check emails or work-related messages and use features like "Do Not Disturb" modes outside of work hours. Consider separate devices or user profiles for work and personal use to reinforce this separation.

Scheduling with Intention: The Power of Planning
Use scheduling to reinforce boundaries. Allocate specific blocks of time for work and protect your personal time with equal rigor. Include breaks, meals, and end times in your schedule, and respect these commitments as you would any work meeting. This intentional planning helps prevent work from bleeding into your personal time.

Communicating Boundaries: The Clarity of Expectations
Clear communication with colleagues, clients, and even family members is crucial in maintaining boundaries. Share your work schedule and availability, and set expectations about response times for communication outside work hours. This clarity helps manage others' expectations and supports your efforts to keep work within its designated time and space.

The Mental Switch: Mindfulness Practices
Mindfulness practices can aid in mentally transitioning between work and personal life. A brief meditation or breathing exercise at the end of the workday can serve as a mental "switch," helping you leave work concerns behind and become more present in your personal life. This mental transition is as crucial as the physical one in maintaining a healthy work-life balance.

Personal Time: Prioritizing Self-Care and Hobbies

Ensure that your personal time is truly personal. Engage in activities that replenish and rejuvenate you, whether it's exercise, hobbies, spending time with loved ones, or simply relaxing. Prioritizing these activities reinforces the importance of your personal time and helps prevent work from encroaching on these moments.

The Unplugging Challenge: Taking Real Breaks

Challenge yourself to periods of complete disconnection from work, especially during weekends and vacations. These breaks are vital for mental and emotional recovery, allowing you to return to work refreshed and with a renewed perspective. True disconnection means setting aside not just the physical tools of work but also mentally releasing work-related thoughts and stresses.

Flexibility Within Boundaries: Adapting to Life's Rhythms

While establishing firm boundaries is important, flexibility is also key. Life's demands can be unpredictable, and there may be times when work and personal life need to blend more seamlessly. The goal is not rigid segregation but a dynamic balance that respects your needs and responsibilities in both spheres.

Reassessing and Adjusting: The Ongoing Process

Finally, remember that establishing work-life boundaries is an ongoing process. Regularly reassess how well your boundaries are working and be open to adjusting them as needed. Your needs and circumstances will evolve, and so too should your strategies for maintaining balance.

By embracing these strategies, you can create a work-life boundary that supports your productivity, preserves your personal time, and fosters a sustainable and fulfilling remote work experience.

Chapter 11: Building a Mindfulness Habit

In the whirlwind of deadlines and responsibilities, mindfulness can be a beacon of calm, bringing clarity, focus, and a sense of peace to our work routine. Building a mindfulness habit is not about adding another task to our busy schedules but about weaving mindful moments into the fabric of our daily lives. This chapter offers practical guidance on making mindfulness an integral part of your work routine, transforming your approach to work and enhancing both your well-being and productivity.

Starting Small: The Power of Mini-Mindfulness Practices

The journey to a mindfulness habit begins with small steps. Integrate mini-mindfulness practices into your day—take a moment to focus on your breath before starting a task, practice mindful listening during meetings, or pause to savor your coffee. These brief pauses to engage fully with the present moment can serve as the building blocks of a more sustained mindfulness practice.

Consistency is Key: Establishing a Routine

Consistency lies at the heart of habit formation. Set aside a specific time each day for a mindfulness practice, whether it's a morning meditation, a midday breathing exercise, or a reflective journaling session at the end of the workday. By anchoring your mindfulness practice in your daily routine, you signal to your brain that this is a priority, reinforcing the habit over time.

Your physical environment can significantly influence your ability to maintain mindfulness. Create a workspace that encourages presence—keep it organized and clutter-free, personalize it with items that inspire calm and focus, and ensure it's conducive to the mindfulness practices you wish to incorporate into your day.

Leveraging Technology Mindfully
While technology can often be a source of distraction, it can also be a powerful ally in building your mindfulness habit. Use apps and tools designed to promote mindfulness, from meditation apps to productivity tools that encourage focused work sessions. Set reminders to take mindful breaks or to engage in a brief mindfulness practice at set intervals throughout your day.

Your breath is a powerful tool for anchoring you in the present moment and can be accessed at any time, regardless of where you are or what you're doing. Develop the habit of using your breath as a tool to return to the present, especially in moments of stress or overwhelm. A few deep, conscious breaths can reset your mental state and bring you back to a place of calm and clarity.

Mindful Eating: Nourishing Body and Mind
Transform meals and snack times into opportunities for mindfulness. Instead of eating at your desk while working, take a proper break to enjoy your food. Pay attention to the flavors, textures, and sensations of eating, turning this into a practice of mindfulness that nourishes both your body and mind.

Mindful movement, such as stretching, yoga, or a short walk, can be a valuable part of your mindfulness habit. Use these activities not only as a break from sitting but as a practice in mindfulness, fully focusing on the sensations in your body and the movement itself, bringing a sense of presence and awareness to the activity.

Reflective Practices: Journaling and Gratitude
End your day with a reflective mindfulness practice. Journaling about your experiences, challenges, and achievements can provide clarity and perspective, while a gratitude practice can shift your focus to the positive aspects of your day. These practices encourage a mindful review of your day, fostering a sense of completion and readiness to transition out of work mode.

Mindfulness in Communication: A Practice in Empathy and Presence
Make mindfulness a part of your communication habits. Practice active listening, give your full attention to the person you're communicating with, and be mindful of your responses. This not only improves the quality of your interactions but also deepens your relationships and fosters a more mindful work environment.

Building a Community of Mindfulness
You don't have to embark on this journey alone. Engage with colleagues or peers who are interested in mindfulness, share practices and experiences, and support each other in building this habit. A community of mindfulness can provide

encouragement, inspiration, and a sense of shared purpose, enhancing the resilience and sustainability of your practice.

Embracing Mindfulness as a Way of Life
Building a mindfulness habit is a journey that extends beyond the confines of your work routine. It's about embracing mindfulness as a way of life, a lens through which you view your experiences, challenges, and interactions. As you weave mindfulness into the tapestry of your daily activities, you'll find it not only transforms your approach to work but enriches your entire life, bringing a deeper sense of purpose, clarity, and well-being to everything you do.

Chapter 12: Mindful Adaptation to Work Challenges

The landscape of work, particularly in a home office setting, is replete with challenges that can test our patience, resilience, and focus. From tight deadlines to communication breakdowns, these hurdles are an inherent part of professional life. Yet, mindfulness offers a powerful toolkit for navigating these challenges, transforming our responses and fostering a sense of calm and clarity in the face of adversity. This chapter delves into strategies for applying mindfulness to overcome common work-related challenges, enhancing our capacity to adapt and thrive.

Tight deadlines can induce stress, narrowing our focus and triggering a fight-or-flight response. Mindfulness counters this by anchoring us in the present, enabling a shift from a reactive to a proactive mindset. When faced with a looming deadline, take a moment to ground yourself with a few deep breaths, focusing solely on the sensation of breathing. This pause can help dissipate stress, allowing you to approach the task with a clear mind and a focused, calm approach.

Overcoming Procrastination with Mindful Awareness
Procrastination is often a response to underlying emotions such as fear, anxiety, or a sense of overwhelm. Mindfulness invites us to observe these emotions without judgment, acknowledging their presence and exploring their roots. By bringing mindful awareness to the act of procrastination, we can gently guide

ourselves back to the task at hand, breaking the cycle of avoidance and engaging with our work with a renewed sense of purpose.

Transforming Stress through Mindful Reframing
Stress is an inevitable aspect of work, but mindfulness offers a pathway to transform our relationship with it. When stress arises, practice mindful reframing by viewing the stressor as an opportunity for growth or learning. This shift in perspective, grounded in present-moment awareness, can alter our emotional and physiological response to stress, enabling us to engage with challenges with resilience and adaptability.

Conflicts, whether with colleagues or clients, can escalate quickly if not handled with care. Mindfulness fosters a non-reactive stance, allowing us to listen actively and empathetically, and to respond with thoughtfulness rather than impulsivity. In moments of conflict, practice pausing before responding, using the breath as a tool to center yourself and approach the situation with a mindset geared towards understanding and resolution.

Change, whether expected or sudden, can be unsettling. Mindfulness encourages an attitude of openness and flexibility, helping us to navigate change with a sense of curiosity rather than resistance. By staying present and grounded, we can better assess new situations, adapt our strategies, and find innovative solutions, turning the challenges of change into opportunities for growth.

Dealing with Distractions: Cultivating Deep Focus

In a world brimming with distractions, especially in a home office, maintaining focus can be a formidable challenge. Mindfulness enhances our ability to recognize distractions without becoming ensnared by them. Regular mindfulness practice, such as meditation, can sharpen our focus, training our minds to return to the task at hand with ease, and fostering a state of flow in our work.

An overwhelming workload can lead to burnout if not managed wisely. Mindfulness aids in mindful prioritization, enabling us to discern the most critical tasks and allocate our energy accordingly. This approach involves a conscious, present-moment assessment of our tasks, guided by our values and goals, ensuring that our efforts are aligned with our most significant priorities.

Cultivating Patience in Long-Term Projects

Long-term projects require sustained effort and patience, qualities that mindfulness can greatly enhance. By focusing on the present step rather than the distant goal, mindfulness helps us find satisfaction in the process, reducing impatience and frustration. Celebrating small milestones and practicing gratitude for the progress made can keep motivation high and make the journey as rewarding as the destination.

Building Resilience through Mindful Acceptance

Resilience, the ability to bounce back from setbacks, is crucial in any professional setting. Mindfulness fosters resilience by promoting acceptance of our current reality, including our challenges and limitations. This acceptance is not passive resignation but a recognition of the present moment from which we can move forward with strength and clarity, using our challenges as stepping stones rather than stumbling blocks.

Embracing Mindfulness as a Catalyst for Growth
Applying mindfulness to work challenges is not about eliminating these challenges but about transforming our relationship with them. By approaching our work with presence, openness, and a non-judgmental attitude, we can navigate even the most turbulent waters with grace. Mindfulness becomes not just a tool for coping but a catalyst for personal and professional growth, enabling us to meet each challenge with resilience, creativity, and a deep sense of calm.

Conclusion

Embarking on the journey to create a mindful and productive home office is a transformative process that melds the serenity of mindfulness with the efficiency of productivity. Through the thoughtful integration of ergonomic setups, mindful rituals, and intentional communication, we can cultivate workspaces that not only foster focus and creativity but also nurture our well-being. The practical exercises, alongside visual aids and a wealth of resources, provide a roadmap to navigate this journey, offering guidance and inspiration every step of the way.

The real-life examples of individuals who have successfully implemented these strategies serve as beacons of possibility, demonstrating that balance is achievable, regardless of the challenges that remote work may present. As we apply these principles to our daily routines, we transform our workspaces into havens of tranquility and efficiency, where professional achievements and personal growth go hand in hand.

In this journey, the ultimate destination is not a fixed point but a continuous evolution towards a more mindful, balanced, and fulfilling work life. By embracing these practices, we open ourselves to the profound impact mindfulness can have on our productivity and overall quality of life, making our home office a place of purpose, peace, and productivity.

Key Takeaways

As we journey through the transformative landscape of creating a serene and efficient home office environment, we've explored a myriad of strategies designed to intertwine mindfulness with productivity. These practices, from establishing a mindful workspace to navigating work challenges with presence and grace, offer a holistic approach to transforming your work-from-home experience. Here, we encapsulate the essence of our journey, distilling the key takeaways that can guide you towards a more mindful, balanced, and fulfilling professional life within the comfort of your home.

Embrace Your Zen Workspace: Begin by crafting a physical environment that supports clarity and calm. Declutter, organize, and infuse your space with elements that promote tranquility and focus, creating a sanctuary where productivity flourishes.

Ergonomic Harmony: Invest in your physical well-being through ergonomic solutions that marry comfort with productivity. This foundation of physical ease is crucial for sustaining mindfulness and efficiency throughout your workday.

Mindful Rituals: Incorporate mindful starting rituals to set a positive tone for your day. Engage in practices that ground you in the present, from breathing exercises to setting intentions, paving the way for a day characterized by focused and meaningful work.

Presence in Productivity: Leverage techniques like the Pomodoro Technique and digital detoxing to cultivate deep focus and presence in your tasks. Embrace the power of single-tasking and mindful breaks to enhance your productivity and well-being.

Communication with Compassion: In the realm of remote work, clear and compassionate communication is key. Practice active listening and empathetic engagement to foster positive relationships and a supportive work environment.

Physical Wellness: Integrate physical activity and healthy habits into your day to counteract the sedentary nature of desk work. From scheduled movement breaks to mindful eating, prioritize your physical health as a cornerstone of productivity.

Work-Life Balance: Establish clear boundaries between your professional and personal life to maintain balance. Use physical cues, rituals, and mindful practices to delineate your workday, ensuring your home remains a place of both productivity and peace.

Building Mindfulness: Cultivate a regular mindfulness practice that becomes woven into the fabric of your daily routine. From mini-mindfulness moments to dedicated meditation sessions, let mindfulness be your constant companion, enhancing focus, resilience, and well-being.

Adapting Mindfully: Approach work challenges with a mindful perspective, using presence, acceptance, and adaptability as tools to navigate obstacles with grace and creativity.

As you stand at the threshold of this mindful journey, remember that the transformation of your home office into a haven of productivity and serenity is an evolving process, one that mirrors your own growth and adaptation. Each step, each strategy, is an invitation to engage more deeply with your work and yourself, fostering an environment where both can thrive.

Embrace these practices not just as tasks to be completed but as pathways to a richer, more connected way of working and living. The journey to a mindful and productive home office is both a destination and a continuous voyage, one that promises a deeper sense of fulfillment, balance, and joy in your professional life. We encourage you to take these steps, to weave mindfulness into the very fabric of your workday, and to embark on this transformative journey with an open heart and a willing spirit.

Case Studies

As we dig deeper into the transformative journey of creating a mindful and productive home office, it's illuminating to explore real-life examples and case studies of individuals from Gen X and Millennials who have successfully integrated these strategies into their lives. These stories not only provide tangible evidence of the practices in action but also offer inspiration and insights that can guide your own journey.

Case Study 1: Emma's Ergonomic Oasis

Emma, a Gen X graphic designer, transformed her chronic discomfort and dwindling productivity by redesigning her workspace with ergonomics in mind. She invested in an adjustable chair and desk, positioned her monitor at eye level, and incorporated a footrest. Emma also introduced a routine of standing and stretching every hour, using a timer as a reminder. This shift not only alleviated her physical discomfort but also significantly enhanced her focus and creativity, leading to a noticeable improvement in her work quality and overall job satisfaction.

Case Study 2: Alex's Mindful Mornings

Alex, a Millennial software developer, found himself overwhelmed by the blur of starting his workday without a clear transition from personal time. He established a mindful morning ritual that included ten minutes of meditation, setting intentions for the day, and a brief gratitude practice. This routine helped Alex enter his workday with a sense of calm, clarity, and purpose, dramatically improving his productivity and reducing feelings of burnout.

Case Study 3: Sofia's Digital Detox Breaks

Sofia, a Gen X content writer, struggled with constant distractions from digital notifications, leading to fragmented focus and mounting stress. She implemented digital detox breaks into her day, dedicating specific times to step away from all electronic devices. During these breaks, Sofia engaged in short walks outside, mindful breathing, or simply enjoying a cup of tea with full presence. This practice allowed her to return to her work refreshed and more focused, significantly enhancing her ability to produce high-quality content under tight deadlines.

Case Study 4: Jordan's Communication Transformation

Jordan, a Millennial project manager, faced challenges in maintaining clear and compassionate communication with his remote team. He began practicing active listening, ensuring he fully understood team members' perspectives before responding. Jordan also made a conscious effort to express empathy and acknowledgment in his digital correspondence. This mindful approach to communication fostered a more positive team dynamic, reduced misunderstandings, and enhanced collaboration on projects.

Case Study 5: Leah's Work-Life Harmony

Leah, a Gen X entrepreneur, found her work life encroaching on her personal time, leading to burnout and diminished personal relationships. She established firm boundaries by creating a designated workspace separate from her living areas and setting clear start and end times for her workday. Leah also developed end-of-day rituals, such as a short walk or reading, to mark the transition from work to personal time. These changes helped Leah regain balance, leading to improved mental health and more quality time spent with family and friends.

These case studies from Gen Xers and Millennials illustrate the profound impact of integrating mindfulness and productivity strategies into the home office. Emma, Alex, Sofia, Jordan, and Leah's stories serve as testaments to the transformative power of these practices, offering both inspiration and practical insights for anyone looking to enhance their work-from-home experience. Let their journeys inspire you to embark on your own path toward a more mindful, balanced, and productive work life.

Practical Exercises

Incorporating practical exercises and productivity hacks into your daily routine can significantly enhance your mindfulness and efficiency in the home office. Here are some tailored activities and strategies designed to cultivate presence and maximize productivity, allowing you to experience the full benefits of a mindful work environment.

Mindfulness Exercises

1. The Five Senses Exercise

Purpose: To ground you in the present moment and sharpen your sensory awareness.

How to Practice: Take a moment to notice:

5 things you can see: Look around your workspace and identify five items, observing their colors, shapes, and textures.

4 things you can feel: Touch four objects and notice their temperature, texture, and weight.

3 things you can hear: Close your eyes and tune into three sounds within your environment, near or far.

2 things you can smell: Identify two scents in your space, whether it's the aroma of your coffee or the scent of your notebook.

1 thing you can taste: Take a sip of a drink or a small bite of food, and focus on the flavors and sensations.

2. Mindful Breathing

Purpose: To center your thoughts and calm your mind.

How to Practice: Sit comfortably, close your eyes, and take deep, slow breaths. Focus solely on the sensation of your breath entering and leaving your body. If your mind wanders, gently bring your attention back to your breath. Practice for 3–5 minutes to start, gradually increasing the duration as you become more comfortable.

Productivity Hacks

1. The Two-Minute Rule

Purpose: To prevent small tasks from piling up and causing overwhelm.

How to Implement: If a task will take two minutes or less to complete, do it immediately. This simple rule can prevent a backlog of minor tasks, keeping your workspace and mind clear.

2. Time Blocking

Purpose: To allocate specific blocks of time for different tasks or types of work, enhancing focus and efficiency.

How to Implement: Divide your workday into blocks of time, each dedicated to a specific task or type of task. For example, reserve mornings for deep work tasks that require concentration and afternoons for meetings and administrative tasks. Use a digital calendar or planner to organize these blocks visually and stick to them as closely as possible.

3. The "One Touch" Email Rule

Purpose: To reduce the time spent managing emails and prevent your inbox from becoming a source of stress.

How to Implement: When you open an email, take immediate action: reply, delete, delegate, or file it. Avoid leaving emails in your inbox to be re-read or dealt with later, as this can lead to unnecessary clutter and repeated handling of the same messages.

By integrating these mindfulness exercises and productivity hacks into your daily routine, you can cultivate a more mindful approach to your work while also streamlining your workflow for maximum efficiency. These practices offer a balanced approach to enhancing your well-being and productivity, allowing you to thrive in your home office environment.

Resources

To further support your journey towards creating a mindful and productive home office, a carefully curated Resources Section can be an invaluable tool. This list includes a variety of apps, books, and websites designed to enhance your mindfulness practice and elevate your productivity. Each resource has been selected for its potential to provide guidance, inspiration, and practical tools that you can integrate into your daily work routine.

Apps for Mindfulness and Productivity

Headspace: A user-friendly app offering guided meditations, mindfulness exercises, and sleep stories to reduce stress and improve focus.

Calm: Known for its wide range of meditation sessions, Calm also includes breathing exercises, sleep stories, and calming music designed to enhance mindfulness.

Forest: An innovative app that encourages productivity by helping you stay focused on tasks while growing a virtual forest, promoting both concentration and environmental awareness.

Todoist: A task management app that helps organize work tasks and personal errands in one place, making it easier to stay on top of your priorities.

Trello: A versatile tool for organizing projects and tasks using boards, lists, and cards, facilitating clear visualization of workflows and collaboration with team members.

Books on Mindfulness and Productivity

"Wherever You Go, There You Are" by Jon Kabat-Zinn: A classic book that introduces the principles of mindfulness and how to incorporate them into daily life, offering insights that are particularly relevant to the home office environment.

"The Miracle of Mindfulness" by Thich Nhat Hanh: This book by the renowned Zen master provides simple yet profound teachings on the art of mindful living, offering practices that can enhance presence and focus in work and life.

"Deep Work: Rules for Focused Success in a Distracted World" by Cal Newport: Newport's book delves into the benefits of deep, uninterrupted work and provides strategies for minimizing distractions to achieve higher productivity, especially pertinent for home office settings.

"Essentialism: The Disciplined Pursuit of Less" by Greg McKeown: Essentialism explores the concept of focusing on what truly matters, eliminating the non-essential, and making the most impactful use of your time and energy.

Websites and Online Resources

Mindful.org: An online resource offering articles, practices, and insights on mindfulness, including ways to integrate mindfulness into your workday and navigate workplace challenges with presence and compassion.

Zen Habits: Created by Leo Babauta, this blog offers practical advice on simplicity, mindfulness, and productivity, with actionable tips for transforming your work habits and creating a mindful work environment.

Lifehacker's "How I Work" Series: This series features interviews with successful professionals about their productivity habits and workspaces, providing real-life inspiration and tips for optimizing your own home office setup.

The Muse: Offering a wide range of articles on productivity, work-life balance, and career development, The Muse is a valuable resource for anyone looking to enhance their work experience, particularly in a remote or home office context.

By exploring these resources, you'll discover a wealth of knowledge and tools at your fingertips, ready to assist you in cultivating a more mindful and efficient work environment. Whether through guided meditations, organizational apps, insightful reads, or inspirational web content, these resources are designed to support you on your journey towards a balanced, productive, and fulfilling home office experience.